MW01539190

Parabola Dreams

Silvia Scheibli and Alan Britt

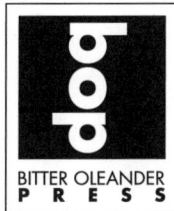

Bitter Oleander Press
Fayetteville, New York

The Bitter Oleander Press
4893 Tall Oaks Drive
Fayetteville, New York 13066-9776 USA

www.bitteroleander.com
info@bitteroleander.com

Copyright ©2013 Silvia Scheibli and Alan Britt

Library of Congress
Control Number 2012950808

ISBN 13: 978-0-9786335-9-2
ISBN 10: 0-9786335-9-8
All rights reserved under International and Pan-American
copyright conventions. No part of this book may be reproduced
except in the case of brief quotations embodied in critical articles
and reviews, stored in a retrieval system, or transmitted in any
form, electronic, mechanical, or other means, now known or
hereafter invented, without written permission of the author.

Joanne Bracken, Editorial Assistant
Typesetting and Layout by Abecedarian Books, Inc.
www.abeced.com
books@abeced.com

Cover design by Deanna Washington
Cover photograph of Silvia Scheibli by Carolyn Johnstone
Cover photgraph of Alan Britt by Charles P. Hayes
Distributed in the United States by *Small Press Distribution*
Berkeley, CA 94710-1409
www.spd.books.org

Printed by McNaughton & Gunn, Inc.
Saline, Michigan 48176
www.bookprinters.com

Manufactured in the United States of America

CONTENTS

PART II
ALAN BRITT
SECTION 1

SECTION 2

Acknowledgments

Grateful acknowledgment to the editors of publications in which many of the poems first appeared:

Ann Arbor Review, Barnwood International Poetry Magazine, The Bitter Oleander, Calliope Nerve, The Cat's Meow for Writers and Readers, Cider Press Review, The Coe Review, Danse Macabre, Deep Tissue Magazine, English Journal, Eskimo Pie, The Gothic: New Jersey City University's Alumni Magazine, Heeltap, Illuminations, Indigo Rising, Leaf Garden Press, Milk Sugar, The Minnesota Review, On Barcelona, pacific REVIEW, Queen's Quarterly (Canada), *Rolling Thunder Quarterly, Sprindrift, Straitjackets, 13th Warrior Review, Tree Killer Ink* (Canada), *Truck,* and *Unlikely 2.0.*

"Hanging Drywall with Gene Manning" featured in Poetry Super Highway's poet of the week for February 25-March 3, 2013, Rick Lupert, editor (http://poetrysuperhighway.com/potw.html).

"Poem Written on a Summer Evening in Maryland" appeared in *Poised in Flight Anthology*, A.J. Huffman and April Salzano, editors, Kind of a Hurricane Press, Daytona Beach, FL: 2013.

"En El Dia de los Muertos - Nogales, Sonora," "The Border," "Flight Across US Border" and "We Are You" included in the We Are You Project International (www.WeAreYouProject.org).

Part I

Silvia Scheibli

Section 1

Breakfast at Eleven –

For Cesar

Two blonde, white-tailed deer
      in mesquite shadow
      very still
      sun-spotted backs
      long tongues reaching for
      new mesquite beans,
Inspire
      to kiss fresh raspberries
Oats & honey
      on your chest.

Sin Agua

Sin agua —
He came to me,
              Bitter
To be by my side.

Sin luna —
    Sin luna blanca
He gave me a carnation.

Con amarillas
   White and yellow
He gave me his life.

Ay,
He gave me his bitter life
Con las
        amarillas blancas
            Y con la musica
I slept with him.

Stands on a Chair

The full moon stands on a chair
Wearing my shoes.

Standing on a chair
With my metallic shoes, the moon
Points at night hawks.

I want your green mask.
I want to lie with you
On the earth with no shadow.

Ay –
Give me your green mask
    And white blood.

I'll never ask for anything
                            again.

Yes –

       I conjure you up so easily.

Your eyes
       Silver olive trees.

       Your
       Gestures.

A peacock's neck,
       In smoky pre-dawn light.

January's Frost Moon

When
the lizard's blood

is just

a drop of silver,

    I would like

        to sleep with the

Frost Moon.

Conservatory of Flowers –
Golden Gate Park

Castle of glass –
       French silk-stained glass
With white smocked bodice,
       Collar & sleeves.

Testimony of our love
       Of Baptisms
At the chalice of
       Crimson orchids.

Orchids' cardinal
Currents do not lie.

Form a radiant wreath
       Of water flowing
Beneath our footsteps.

Japanese Tea Garden –
Golden Gate Park

Cherry blossoms are really white,
As white and curved as the
Half moons of Marlena's toenails.

She does not know it yet, only suspects
there are dreams hiding among the trees.

Words among the leaves
dressed in a christening gown,
Whisper mother secrets.

She watches our open faces.

Japanese Tea Ceremony –
Golden Gate Park

Elegy for June Morrall, 1948-2010

The traditional tea ceremony
        embodies the essence of bamboo.

Vital essence
      for the one drinking not only the jasmine tea,
But also
      the floor, walls and lanterns.

The drinkers pour simplicity   into a tiny cup
        and are transformed
By a
Swallow's flight   at their fingertips.

Those who usually reach out   suddenly
Reach in
      with the singular gesture
Of a night heron on lips.

Moon Rise –

For Marlena Angelina Lisac

Tonight
the full moon
arrived
      in a carriage.

Searching for the girl
with denim
blue eyes.

Splashed diamonds
on her clover
      honey hair.

Tonight
the full moon
arrived
      in a carriage.

Lace
      curtains
            opened wide.

Half Moon –

For Kayla Adriana Petrovic

The half moon
  Directly above me
Framed by palm fronds
    Splits me in half, too.
My arms spread out
        Embrace the sky.
I reach out
    Beyond what I know
Beyond what I feel
Beyond everything left in the past
To something unknown and new
And sweet as your full lips,
Tiny fingers.

    In the bond defining us
We are here
In this universe,
Defining us.

Be this moon,
    Be these palms, Be these fronds.
Be this sky
        Splitting us in half.
Be the shape of this moon.

En El Dia de los Muertos –
Nogales, Sonora, Mexico

Death
Sat on a chair
At Pancho Villa's Bar,
Sipping
        Cappucino kisses.

Guests nodded
In her direction, as
Passers-by quickened
Their steps.

En el Dia de los Muertos
In a low-cut gown
Death
Was content
        At Pancho's.

Three Days After Christmas

Santa was at Pancho's Mall
On Avenida Obregon,
      Nogales, Sonora.

There with his new
Pungent perfume,
      He looked for his next
Shot of Patron.

Duke women beat Connecticut.

A vendor reminded us that
Baby Boomers pay less
      And that Salon Regis is a metaphor

For Margaritas Sabrosas.

The Border

We did not cross the border,
The border crossed us.

      —Dolores Huerta

I gaze river-like
Looking for a river
 or even some tree ducks
But there is only this endless
Late afternoon freight train,
   rumbling through the intersection.
Brakes squealing.
Rolling to a stop.

On my left Mesquite bushes
   crouch
    float up the clearing
    and melt
In between cracks of boxcars.

Moving again,
Dim amber lights flicker
& jolt
On the track.

River-like
I scan the empty road.

Parabolas –

For Alan Britt

Rilke wrote poems
To understand his
Spiritual self.

An Apache holy man said,
Each person has two selves –
The physical one
And the spiritual one,
Who need to make friends.

In the Middle Ages
Every knight needed a poem
To be taken seriously
By his ladylove.

Taoists found poems
Are as necessary
As a good kitchen knife.

Rumi said poems
are the only true language
God understands, and
Mira Bai
Wrote seductive poems
To her god, Krishna.

Shakespeare wrote
154 love sonnets
To carpe diem.

Lorca wrote
Poems
To die.

Flight Across the US Border

There was a black butterfly.

She saw it.
Right away, she saw it.

She begged her son
Not to cry.
To be still.

To hide it.
  Under his tongue.

But she saw it immediately —
Fiery
    Red ants carried it off.

While in Search of
the Rose-throated Becard

Claude Debussy's libretto of Pelleas and Melisande
And Verdi's I Due Foscari,
I came across a penumbra of headlines that
Crystallized our planet's death wish.

Headlines such as –

Iran rejects US condition for nuclear talks.

General orders troops to undergo training
      In core moral values.

Angry girlfriends turn to Web for revenge.

These headlines were followed by analyses of
               Whys and hows,
And I couldn't keep on reading this.

So, I turned away –
     Turned in the direction of the five quail rushing
To keep up with their mother and father
             At the water dish.

Myth of the Dream Maker

Today I dreamed of hundreds of red crabs
Crawling under and over seaweed covered rocks
To reach the foam of the sea.

Yesterday I dreamt of a woman
Whose heart was tied in rags
Sitting on the cliff above the same
Seaweed covered rocks,
But she was waiting for another dream.

As she waited and waited
The rags around her heart became undone
And her exposed heart was transformed into
One red crab who joined the others
Crawling over the seaweed covered shore
To reach the foam of the sea.

Memory of a Small Brown Bird
in the Garden in Rahlstedt

My sleep
    was a spinning top –
        garish colors
Chasing each other.

I was afraid
I would not recognize my surroundings,
and wake up a stranger to my own perceptions.

I began to stare at sentences,
    eavesdrop on words.

Sometimes I sensed their meaning
    dressed in chiffon clouds.

The small, brown bird
    that disappeared inside
the pear tree
    when I was five,

Exists.

It is dressed in my words.

Good-Night Bird

Listen to the golden eye
        whistle from the casita roof,
Or is she in the twin palms now?
     Too dark to see.
I imitate her voice.
The high-pitched sound makes me real.

I've always liked the phrase,
    "Bend it like Beckham."

It reminds me of how reality shifts
    From one spot
To another   effortlessly.

Exhaling helps.
So does glancing at a Saguaro with
    Chili seedlings sprouting around it.
How it happens is irrelevant.
    It does.
Sometimes without warning.

Green Mask

My hands appear to be wearing
  The green mask of a Buddha.

Palms reflect a friendly smile.

I would like the key, I say.
She tells me that I already have it.

Stockings –

For Toulouse Lautrec

It seems odd and sad
I never noticed.

I never really knew or felt anything
Until you finally stopped me
        With your black stockings.

Deeply wooly and
Bottomless,
        Burning with light.

Section 2

No Rain for Five Months

Then suddenly
     the earth smells like
Mango popsicles.

The water jumps
  a good foot off the pavement
     sizzling like fat.

My skin that tasted
     like straw all this time
  begins to feel
like banana leaves.

Javalina growl
      in Comoro Canyon
    shoving bellies into mud.

Blood red cactus flowers
   open windows.

Waiting for Rain —
with Duane Locke's "sonic texture of words"

Crickets
Drink coffee
In a corner
Under blue magueys.

Fat lizards
Sculpted collars
Spill
Over shoulders.

Inca dove
Stares through
Her blue mask—
Red eye hooked on
Ristras.

Hooded orioles
Suddenly sink,
Disappear
In a mandolin
Canopy.

Sulphur butterflies
Glimmer.

In secret
A varied bunting rattles
Coral mesquite
Beans.

A pair of bronze
Swallows

Ties
Hair
In knots.

The overture lingers.

The rain does not
Delay.

On the First Day of Monsoon Season

Nude
Banana leaves
Scissor-kick
Light
Across
Saltillo tiles

Terracotta suns
Bask
On ponds

Goldfish swallow
Hours
In one gulp

Blue-throated, male
Hummingbirds
Unzip heat –
Buzz females

Red hibiscus
Point a finger
Indicating rain

Coyote
Teeth-marks
Stalk
Red yucca

One fat
White lizard
Waits upside down
On stucco

Flamboyant
Orange tarantula
Crawls
Over
Myrtle

Mornings
Have no end
And no beginning

Only thunderheads
Flicking a veil
Back and forth
Patiently

Later
Nude banana leaves
Take up
Green masks

The pond's surface
Is spotted silver
With rain

Goldfish
Nibble

On spider web
Lightning

A red hibiscus
Dies

Coyotes
Lick
Blue agaves

White lizards
Catch red flies
On caramel
Stucco

Mornings
Have no beginnings
Other than
Clouds
Flashing tail lights –

        Illuminating
Raindrops

Muddy Days

There will be days
Without monsoons.

Worthless days without
A full Thunder Moon.

Then there will be days with mud.

Muddy days.

Nervous
Leopard frogs
     in cattle ponds
     ready to migrate
     to a new water source
     or
     dive for cover.

I prefer muddy days.

Instantly It Will Rain Again

When it starts
      The dove's lilac eyeliner
Will smear.

Shortly,
  Sand itself will bleed and
Ignite a
      Thousand candles.

But the rain's face will
      remain forever invisible.

Except that somewhere,
      it is always on the verge
of being recognized.

When I looked at the lizard's
      yellow eye
      just now
I felt hard drops
      the second his collar
      disappeared in the brown skin
Of a stone.

The stone darkened –
      The air breathed much lighter.

Been Ironing All Day

Trying to eliminate creases
      Made by glib, off-hand comments.

Starching the tone has not helped,
      And the best posture is nowhere
To be seen.

I squeak —
      Like a novice clarinet player.

Where is the damn rain?

Sinagua Ruins —
Sedona, Arizona

Closest
To the turquoise moon
        and copper ponies —
   a silver falcon
Shoots across the gulch.

Spirit does not investigate,
does not lie.
      Lives in green lace,
Red granite, and
Red limestone shoulders.

Makes the sound of the hawk,
        but is not the hawk.

Screeches only
     at the turquoise moon.
Nothing else matters.

Sinagua ruins consist of untold stories,
Many times
      silent —

     Not holding their breath,
Giving away nothing,
Except when it rains.

     Then stones speak of dark eyelids,
Squinting.

Wet Cheeks on Cactus

The cactus in front of me
       is an acrobat
who wishes he were
       the long white streaks
down the black chin
         of a desert sparrow.

This small gray bird
       finds water,
splash of tides,
steps through foam,
       feet sunk in wet sand.

While the cactus
 waits
       imagines wet
cheeks.

Ghost Orchid

The blood of the orchid
Was white,

Like rain
With the scent of figs.

The ghost orchid
Stood still,

On the earth
With no shadow.

Sea foam oozed
From my fingers.

A Real Place

Early afternoon
   I dozed
        like a tightly curled banana leaf.

When the monsoon entangles the imagination
Lightening graphs eyebrows on marigolds.

A young oriole stays
Close to her nest.

Later
       when the humidity walks in
Shaking hands
         I unfold my dream quietly.
  Rethink my address. Wonder   if
This place is still real.

Song of the Scorpion

On entering
open lips
of the lily
the scorpion
caresses
the arch of the night.

Love of mesquites,
tides, oranges
and melody of kisses
has brought him here.

In the amber night
the scorpion
brown and brittle
yearns to escape.

Kokopelli

Every artist has his stigma.
—Fini Locke

Kokopelli, god of
Artists, poets and musicians
Sees
Our planet
With blue eyes.

Through transparent
Blue eyelids.

Sees invisible
Blue lips

Kissing
The
Invisible
Blue.

Elegy for Koi –
    Lago Corte

Two lizards
        Track a dark tequila moon –

Two cupped breasts
Crouch in the bowl
        Of a horned moon –

Two golden-red koi
Rub against
        Memory's brick wall.

Multiple Choice

"Blue eye ring,
                      coral-lilac
iridescent throat."

A new martini?

New cocktail glass?

Lipstick, eyeliner?

Or

                Centuries old mourning dove?

Saffron Finch –
Hanalei, Hawaii

Saffron finch
      in a mesh of vines,
Mist and tree ferns.

      Flight without words.

Beams of saffron light
          rising through
damp, lacy foliage.

Brown as a Potato

I remind him to look for a spotted brown bird
     When we search for the varied bunting female.

Just off the ground in a tiny cup of twigs
     In the crepe myrtle or mesquite.

I want to paint the mesquite beans
A reflective gold,
Like the antique hands of a clock,
     Telling us what month it is.

The varied buntings nest in early August.

Have You Noticed

An oriole's strumming
Or a cicada's castanets

Silent stone
Or flower

Even air and mud
Burn brighter

When hummingbirds kiss?

No Moon over Rio Rico

Only silver gourds with
Rose-red impressions scattered on sand.

Only ponies
Licking shiny paw prints at dusk.

Only Miro-red cardinals in mesquites.

Only giant grasshoppers with
Rouged mandibles on pavement.

Only zinfandel butterflies eating chitalpa.

Only spotted, terra-cotta toads
Waiting to be born.

Only fuchsia tarantulas,
Fluorescent wall lizards,
Cranberry ocotillo,
But no moon.

Only raspberry wasps,
Cayenne lightning,
Turmeric moss
And bats.

But no moon,
Over Rio Rico.

Night Blooming Cereus

Adobe doves
Flashed wings
And tails
Like lace curtains.

At once
       White hammerheads
       White armadillos
       White orchids
Raced across the sky.

A black vulture
Raised desire
Like a dark spinnaker
In my skin.

Agaves wept.

Blue Matisse horses
Lifted heads into the air.

       Kokopelli's blue flute
Exploded.

Ocotillo bones
Chile ristras
Red geraniums
       Tasted love.

The scent tied my limbs
In green ribbons

Part II

Alan Britt

Section 1

Girl in Yellow

This morning your breasts were frozen
tulips & your eyes, well, clearly you
wear contacts, watery jade contacts,
for what purpose, I can't say,
but you must've overheard.

Light through library curtain
frames you like Fragonard's La Liseuse,
pensive, palpitating beneath your
21st-century canary gown's
dirty secrets hidden between
white satin folds.

Clearly you were that girl in yellow
reading the verses of obscure poets
as though they were sacred hymns.

With Time to Kill in the Midst of a Crisis

For 20 years I've never quite discerned
these twisted white flowers
in twilight that filters
our gauze dining room curtains.

Outside, heavy humidity rubs her breasts
against all eight window panes.

I believe these white flowers
belong to the camellia or wild rose
family, somehow,
flapping their crocheted wings
at the sight of April
sauntering in the nude
past our open dining room window.

Ode to Maple Seeds

(For Michelangelo Buonarroti)

Maple seeds fall to the ground,
spiraling toward their heaven
that determines whether they survive and flourish
into full-grown maple trees
or disperse their atoms
for alternate purposes.

Same thing for humans,
only we float skyward
to our heaven,
which we'll never see
and never touch.

Spanish Wine in Early Summer

This Spanish wine
has all the dryness
of rattlesnake skin
shed between the forked thoughts
of an Arizona moon.

Moon's left elbow
tinged with bruises.

If this wine
truly is snake,
then its warm scales
are deep kisses
pressed by a complete stranger
against the lips of last night's dream.

This wine wears a loose-fitting robe
while she writes
of loneliness
on pages made from parchment
and pearls
in her adolescent diary.

Poem Written on a Summer Evening in Maryland

This blank page,
a dirty white feather
discarded
by mute swan
against
smooth
soapstone.

At sunrise,
the swan's shadow
glides
across shallow
brackish bay water.

Currents of death
flowing
through
the swan's webbed feet
caress
a mourning dove's
crushed trumpet.

The Downy Woodpecker

After fourteen long, lean years,
the downy woodpecker finally returns
two days in a row!

On the underside of logic,
defying gravity,
white gunsmoke
dusting black feathers,
Archbishop's red cap
tilted back.

A speckled delight!

I lower the curtain;
its gauze falls
like ice
turned to kisses.

Contemplating Summer

Thoughts are lovers
massaging skin
until it flinches.

Metaphysical breath
untangles bones
of consciousness.

And the body
heaves
as though it's just seen god
forcing his way
through the iron gates
of hell.

Neighborhood Dogs Have It Easy Tonight

Neighborhood dogs are thick tonight.

The rough collie on Janet Road
wears a serape
courtesy of shamans
who roam our streets
every other Wednesday evening.

Her serape
a symbol
of canine emancipation,
freedom
from the terracotta
eyelids
of human intervention.

Our neighborhood is grateful
for any opportunity
to showcase
its lime breezes,
its rose-of-Sharon
tumbling
like lavender gypsies
over the bare shoulders
of split-rail fences.

By now neighborhood dogs, almost asleep,
enjoy a cool vent beside a basement door,
or else roam the den
looking for scraps

of bologna,
pizza crust,
or a pale hand with magenta fingernails
to stroke the thin contours
of a lower jaw bone.

Genesis in This Day and Age

(Language always searches for its next experience!)
—a squashed blackberry

I love every cucumber,
each yellow squash
whose sticky pollen
intersects my dreams.

The hipbones
of intellect,
lovers themselves
in this garden,
are catbirds rooting
through
banana peppers.

Dusk crawls
over the large, wrinkled shoulder
of a nearby rhubarb.

Blond sunlight
heaves
desperate millenniums
into my
fertile imagination.

Summer Rains on the Garden

After soaking rain,
earthworms bob the surface.

As they gulp fresh air,
robins gulp them.

Crow stumbles into the arena.

Followed by catbird, cardinal,
several finches and blazing oriole.

Some forage for anything edible,
some only seeds,
and some gorge on fat black crickets,
tiny grey-striped spiders
and moths too limp to flee.

Thick maples drip the brew
that washes everything down.

Picking Cucumbers

The other day a tendril
circled my wrist
as I reached for a cucumber.

I paused.

Paring knife in one hand,
tendril in the other.

I admired the yellow squash's patience
producing any number
of sagging orange trumpets.

I inhaled green chilies
turned upside down,
filling their adolescent bellies
with gunpowder.

I marveled at tiny slugs
like drips of mud
between cabbages' whitegreen leaves.

I tasted
lusty red tomatoes
waltzing
a sudden July breeze,
plus military rows
of white asparagus
marching under moonlight.

I even quoted a fairy tale,
the one about Cinderella
chasing her midnight pumpkin
down lamp-lit cobblestones.

At that precise moment I felt
the tendril
loosen
my wrist
and slowly embrace
the splintered bark
of a faded brown tomato stake.

Solitary Night of the Heat Wave

Heavy fireflies
follow
the extreme heat
index
of 102°.

The Irish streetlamp,
her abalone light
falling
in onion skin slices,
reclines naked
against nihilistic humidity.

The streetlamp's mahogany hair
streaked
with white gesso
shatters the large bones
of a split-rail fence.

Jetliners
open stitches
in humid darkness.

August Dreams

Carp devour slick dreams.

Dreams are indigent thoughts.

Dreams cannot be trusted
as they twist black seaweed
around the Atlantic's muscular thighs.

Lovers and psychologists each
have an opinion about dreams.

But lovers and psychologists
rarely agree on anything.

So, dreams go on rocking the Atlantic
like buoys strung together
for the tired tugs
dragging our daily lives into port.

Ode to Guilty Pleasures

Guilty pleasures row gondolas
through the moon's unbuttoned nightgown,
rippling a canal's bare shoulders.

Cicadas and woodpeckers chatter.

Stars etch jellyfish light across an August sky.

Golden tomatoes moan.

Crickets, large drops of crude, digest
magnesium bites from night's humid torso.

Hanging Drywall with Gene Manning

You ripped the board down
just like you said you would.

So, we held it again with the tops
of our calloused skulls, sweltering, trembling
within a nano-inch of fainting.

Then quietly you nailed that soft board,
every square inch on your aluminum stilts
until perfection was yours,
like squeezing the impossible from a finite 4 by 8 foot,
shoehorned piece of perfect puzzle
exactly the way you promised you would,
the way our trembling, sagging asses
hoped you would.

You were Merlin the Magician on stilts;
we knew that from the get-go,
the day we joined the Gene Manning legend,
West Palm Beach, 1967, the infamous
Summer of Love, the summer
of perfect drywall.

Nuns

So, fire's proof enough?

That's it?

After years of incarceration,
I want what's mine.

Warehouse windows shatter.

Tonight, the moon's a Romanian grandmother
with a sterling-tipped, twisted, black cane
poised to crack your skull.

Although nuns, like pigeons, routinely gather
to protect the sacred graveyards,
several nuns were spotted earlier today,
cruising South Dixie Highway in a 1956 T-Bird,
top down, sans opera window.

Their old habits
billowing
in the wind.

Section 2

Ode to September

Chilly wind's manta belly
undulates the blue sky,
if you're down
looking up.

Nearby ambulance displays white teeth
and bad disposition.

Volunteer fire alarm
suddenly ignites the sleepy neighborhood's match head,
then gradually burns down.

Crows leave hair-line cracks in the overcast afternoon.

Their squawks
crumble
the filthy, white porcelain feet
of my patio chair.

Autumn Wasps

Wasps surround your floppy straw
bonnet this early afternoon.

Each striped thorax
resembles dying sunlight.

As you shake your walnut hair,
wasps bob like tassels the bonnet's edge.

A middle-aged poet in Habana
dreams beneath a 36" fluorescent tube.

You shake your walnut hair again.

Wrinkled legs follow you
inside the apartment of that poet
scribbling poems in Habana.

You share a bottle of Australian shiraz
and talk about the old days.

Ode to Velasquez

(For José Rodeiro)

A painter posing before the beveled mirror
of a bustling palace
has the dark look of curious confidence.

Nearby
women flow
across the parquet palace floor.

All the velvet alone that day
must've been worth thousands,
perhaps millions by today's standard.

Velasquez brushes plum blossoms
from the sultry lap
of daily royal existence.

He faces the mirror,
then steps through 500 years to smell
Cuban coffee brewing in José's kitchen.

Ode to 1958

A disillusioned teacher juggles egos
at the Palm Beach County Fair,
1958.

He flips torches,
eats fire,
then burns all the important papers
at the county court house.

The Lobster Man
and the Lobster Man's daughter
dine at a seafood restaurant
somewhere off Military Trail.

My brother,
youngest polo player in the history
of Palm Beach County,
scores the winning goal,
achieves stardom
at the impressionable age of 16.

Then, poetry, ah, the toughest teacher of all
stops by to share a cigarette.

Loosens the silk buttons of her silk blouse,
leans close to breathe elusive wisdom into his ear.

Then Steve discards his saddle,
lays down his bridle one last time
and embraces poetry's eight arms of an Indian goddess

who knows just how elusive wisdom can be
without her web of mythology
nearby to catch it.

Ode to Paradox

(For Silvia Scheibli)

The paradox eventually becomes a simple concept
once you gain insight, and suddenly you feel you

should've known it all along. Like an avocado's wrinkled,
black skin lining the bottom of an ocean green,

Tupperware compost bowl, the paradox stores maple
seeds in its lungs about to burst after two and a half days

of constant rain. Ah, but your lusty dreams shed their silk
scales long ago between the furious nettles growing

along the flaming white sands of the Mojave!

Ode to Langston Hughes

You gotta understand,
that's how he lived,
perhaps the first Beat
to strut the sidewalks
of Harlem.

Well, there was Whitman,
then Lorca came along.

But Langston always saw something unique
in a blindfolded world
that tormented him so.

His poems were rubies
smashed against the wall of fate
in a bigoted crap game.

His voice was a crow
stuffed in the silk breast pocket
of misery.

His poems were shards
of blood spattered
all over the huge, white hands
of America.

Dreams

(For Chanelle Vida Britt: 1993-2004)

> ...*the river*
> *which as it grows deeper*
> *is seen to run slower, clearer.*
>   --Miguel Hernández

Ever notice how dreams
each passing hour, day,
month, year disintegrate
as though eaten voraciously
by piranha or algae?

I suppose that makes perfect sense;
otherwise, we'd be overcome by dreams.

Where could we store
all those dreams?

In shoeboxes
stacked like designer bricks
across the top shelves
of our closets?

We're overrun by boxes!

But these dreams
could be useful,
what with the price of Cable
constantly rising.

We need a back-up plan!

I'm telling you,
we should devise a convenient place
to store our dreams,
so that we might recall them,
reactivate them as necessary
on our most dismal of nights,
on our saddest of nights,
on a night with shallow breathing
through the leafless maples,
on a night with melancholy shoulders
like tonight.

Communal Love

(For Ruxandra Cesereanu)

First, the French doors click,
then my bones,
and suddenly lights flicker
like a spirit tangled
in low ceiling fixtures
while passing through this basement room.

The guitar is purely Mexican.

The guitarist's fingers
tarantulas
tugging the pouting lips
of the senora cantata.

The sound of piano keys
ice falling
from a wedding veil.

This ice quickly scooped
from the glistening counter
by a swift palm,
by elaborate machine guns.

In any event, the mistress
approaches the neon-lit bar
with a swagger
and melting stars on her shoulders.

Death looks her straight in the eyes
and she doesn't even flinch.

Wild Parakeets of Florida

(For Duane Locke)

He parted the wall
so that we could enter.

He melted mortar from the bricks
supporting our future superstitions.

Ultimately, this allowed us to enter.

But, once inside,
we realized that genocide is a disease
more rampant than AIDS,
genocide as ancient as DNA.

And now we're petitioning
what new stadium, exactly,
which new sports franchise,
while our children
slumped in overcrowded classrooms
are herded by underpaid sheepdogs?

This can't be why Blake
parted the Red Sea.

I'm telling you,
Blake was an escaped convict
from the 18th Century
with nowhere else to go.

He reminds me of a poet
who once watched pale blue parakeets
blistering the pine trees
of St. Petersburg, Florida, 1969.

Ode to James Wright

We read James Wright's poem in class today,
the one about him lying in a hammock
listening to cowbells, detailing dragonflies,
wasting his life.

Student response was robust.

In the south corner of our room,
John Keats engaged in conversation
with Wordsworth; I wanted to be there
but was interrupted by Shakespeare,
Aleixandre and Neruda
conversing beneath a thatched veranda
in Lake Worth, Florida.

Later, as James rolled from his hammock,
students followed him
to a fence along a pasture
where his Indian pony awaited them
with the patience of Saint Judas.

In Love with the Universe

I need to back down
this ladder,
this extension ladder leaning
against a yellow grapefruit tree
sheltered by the dirty green hair
of Spanish moss dripping
from Tampa pines.

Why I need to back down
remains a mystery.

But I'll back down just the same
if you promise
to uphold your end
of the bargain.

No more vengeful wars,
and no more former hostages
sporting purple hearts
while escorting grieving First Ladies
who to this day mistrust the wild
but steady hands
of delinquent poets
still in love with the universe.

Iron Tail

♥

Straw-haired, braless,
aureoles like silver dollars
clinking two bits, angelic dimes
& Chief Iron Tail nickels
for the airport taxi.

Leather luggage
scuffing nylon hips & thighs.

We're off!

We're on.

We're off again!

Then we're on
just when we thought.

♥ ♥

What breath
harvested from horseshoes
makes a living spitting houseflies?

Indeed, oxygen turns to sulfur
inside a water buffalo esophagus
when three lionesses flank his final escape,
whether you're an arthritic water buffalo
or a scratchy 1927 Yankees scoreboard,
runs, hits & errors rotated by hand.

♥ ♥ ♥

So it is. Soy-yo-yo-yo.
Soy-yo-yo-yo. Soy-yo-yo-yo.

♥ ♥ ♥ ♥

Mosquitoes cart the head of George Carlin
on their way to the Federal Reserve.

Forgetting to deposit George's head
in nearest FedEx receptacle,
they hide it
inside a lunchbox with generic rocket ship
thermos rattling its retaining wire,
leaking creamy fluid
& belching the faces of nuns
who had better things to do
than babysit this Cretan,
more important matters to attend.

♥ ♥ ♥ ♥ ♥

Spectacular ballerinas
with spectacular pink hearts
beneath dusty footlights
weaving silk heart prints
on drunkest patrons
sweltering
beneath long, skinny rows
of whale torch lights.

A Pleasing Italian Wine

This dry Italian wine
like bones clicking cobblestone.

Hips and knees
twisted into a Cubist frieze.

Eventually, this wine eases
atop a plum velvet cushion
before an ebony baby grand.

Tosses back her long strands of midnight rust
and begins to play
Chopin's Ballade No. 2 in F major.

Trail of Tears x E=MC²

Now dead for generations,
how many trails of tears were there?

Don't source Wikipedia.

Genocide is a bad word, no longer PC.

Each death step, each patch of the quilt,
oops, there goes another infant strapped
to grandmother bequeathing life
to her daughter's newborn son,
another five miles, or who knows what,
but family members have been falling
like flies. So, go forth, go forth,
go forth another twenty-five paces.....
a hundred frozen paces; you,
my darlings, go forth another 700 miles,
or so, & then I'll, I'll eat this
frozen, lifeless aching in my bones,
the final answer to what
I expected to be a warm, colorful swatch
of life I could bequeath
one day to granddaughters & grandsons,
because, hopefully, like you,
they'll already have fallen head-over-heels
in love with our mysterious universe.

Gnossienne

(After Erik Satie)

What is this breeze that isn't a breeze,
this sandpaper light falling from basement fixtures,
light falling like skin without a body, without bones
to give it humanity, bodiless, helpless,
stranded like melancholy, stranded like banana whales
beaching themselves upon the dingy shag carpet,
these molded plastic storage containers with white lids,
empty containers crippled by notebooks and books,
books with black spines, purple spines,
hardbound books the color of young spruce trees,
notebooks with metal spirals of frozen smoke,
spines like metal spirals of frozen smoke,
notebooks with metal spines whose
frozen smoke imprisons the hours circling
above white clocks, hours circling
like buzzards riding the thermals,
hours circling alien clocks and riding
the thermals that aren't really thermals,
circling the light that falls like sandpaper
from the huge bucket of the sun,
light falling like skin, bodiless, boneless skin.

Daisy Jopling Plays the Classics

Honey hardens into crystal.

Antelopes of light leap from your skin.

Violin rocks a cradle on a cliff,
then ignites a 20-mile fuse soaked
in kerosene with a lemon twist.

Cloudy cranes drift down one by one
injecting ink into the river.

Thunder goes to satin & satin to crystal
thorn bushes & from there who knows—
a blue wind with a rose between its teeth,
a grandmother with scorpion kisses,
a hive of lost souls buzzing to go home,
buzzing for cocktails, buzzing for the sake
of buzzing while a little Roma dodges
cobblestone puddles, moonlit puddles
reflecting ice, the cruelest mirror.

Smoke does its cobra dance while juggling
razorblades in a hurricane.

Then orchids for eyes, pearly white
with a discharge of ruby that bleeds
two bodies together, bodies made of lava,
yellow diamonds & silk.

Listening to Lila Downs

Sandalwood stick burns like a torch
feathering a black tsunami above the chasm.

Lila follows los pobrecitos down cobblestone allies
past thundering Civil War Gatling guns wheeled
by US mercenaries masquerading on Halloween—
mercenaries, paid in full by lusty marijuana,
blasting pure and simple folk hoodwinked by the wicked.

Lila, melancholy viper, naked, spotted,
constricting the bruised moon.

Lila, burning the Psalms, Leviticus,
and gospels of the new world order.

Lila, amphibian eclipse of Scorpio.

Lila, mariposa blanca del mundo!

Listening to Paco de Lucía

Something tells me this is serious—
crystal guitar notes
splintering a single squash flower
& scrambling six kaleidoscope mirrors
with cuckoo eggs
before electrocuting Mercutio, thus changing
the world forever.

These notes like sewing needles
or weaving hooks, these notes
taking out the garbage,
juggling wasps of jealousy,
these notes geese taken down
by leaden pellets,
these notes electric suspenders,
these notes, these notes, these notes
piano wires like baby crocodiles snapping
dragonflies & cornflake moths,
these notes............a frog walks
into a bar & says, *Drinks on me!*

Bartender says, *That's great!*
What're you drinking?

Frog says, *Mercury-infested, nuclear-contaminated,*
human excrement pond scum.

101

Ebb & Flow

So, the earth wobbles;
mud escapes
its universal womb.

That's it?

Broken window
stained with transmission fluid.

Cold, cold room,
ice-blue sheets
snapped to attention.

Wine cork
imprinted with counterfeit coat of arms,
or tarantula,
albeit speck spider sized, but a tarantula
all the same.

Ha! The same damnations
that fueled Little Boy
fuel you & me
this very moment.

The same, pure O_2 molecules
that haunted Plato deep in his cave.

The same exhausted atoms from T. rex
after a glorious bloodbath
leaving Triceratops ribs for the Aeolian wind

to fan its bruised sonata
across the wrist, the Christian wrist,
the bare wrist of truth, the wrist
most likely to get nailed, the wrist
seeking art, as though art
could save the universe?

Oh, dear.

The onion sings its song.

Under Ceauçescu that onion was an apple.

We Are You

We rise on jaguar wings orbiting
a bronze waist before crossing
the torch of Liberty.

We sling ruthless reds, bruised
golds & tropical greens across
hurricanes chewing the Atlantic
coast off Cuba.

We surface the Amazon
with webbed toes.

Freedom's eyeglasses fogged we
enter each holy house as though
entering a proverbial hall of mirrors,
aware the moon nursing Manhattan
skyscrapers also splinters the icy peaks
of Peru, ignites Caymans in Columbia
the Quichua in Ecuador, yucca lightning
in Mexico, plus Bolívar's bones in Venezuela.

We chase amnesia thermals, sometimes,
but mostly we prefer heirloom tomatoes,
lean meats, exotic spices, multigrains
& a dozen-year-old California Syrah
after an exhausting day of painting our
dreams across a canvas called America.

Birds of Smoke

A smooth fern curls
above your cabernet.

Behind you a faded tapestry
in which a royal family
practices falconry
outside the oblivious forest.

The Queen's arm extends
toward heaven—
a domesticated falcon
her torch.

The waiter arrives,
glides over your perfumed shoulder,
reveals to glistening eyes
a glazed duck beneath silver.

From your coy lips
trail birds of smoke.

Silvia Scheibli

Photo by Roy Rodriguez

Five Questions for Silvia Scheibli:

1) You are one of the original Immanentist poets. Linguistic Reality which morphed into Immanentism flourished in the late 60's and throughout the 70's. Many of your poems today still exhibit Immanentist qualities. What does Immanentism mean to you?

SS: *Linguistic Reality or Immanentism came as a natural way of writing for me. I was in the right place at the right time surrounded by writers and artists at the University of Tampa, Florida who found an immediate and new approach of communicating that both challenged and compelled us to perceive and interpret the world around us. Imagination held us by the hand and drew us forward in a direction we could not resist. We were head-over-heels in love with creating a new language, an experiential language that fused the poet with nature, and this movement was a means of fermenting our hearts and minds and committing us to creating poems until death do us part.*

2) You've lived in Germany, Florida, California's Mojave Desert and Arizona. Has one environment exerted more influence than another on your poetry?

SS: *I find an aria by Puccini or Mozart just as exciting as a hummingbird's mating dance. The cosmopolitan aspects of a great city such as San Francisco inspire me as much as the sacred environment of the desert or the tropics. Both open my sensibilities and compel me to write.*

3) You are family oriented which has you traveling out-of-state often to attend birthdays, weddings, births, etc. How do you juggle your responsibilities to find time to write?

SS: *Yes, I have been blessed with two wonderful daughters and four adorable grandchildren whom I visit often. One of my favorite poems is "A Child's Christmas in Wales" by Dylan Thomas. This poem fills me with an immediate sense that writing is indeed important to the different generations. That poetry does not only appeal to the esoteric few alone, but also to the heart of each one of us.*

4) Like the great French poet, Yves Bonnefoy, you tend to write in spurts, producing an entire manuscript or so in a matter of weeks and then not writing for months. What inspires you to enter these infrequent zones of explosive creativity?

SS: *Yes, I agree with you that my creativity is sporadic. Sometimes I can hardly stop writing, and other times I just want to stay quiet. Writing for me is always plagued by uncertainty. Sometimes what I want to say is unachievable. Sometimes what I write surprises me. Imagination can be euphoric, daunting, intimidating—a way of facing truths that may be very dark and isolating.*

5) You are sensitive to a variety of social injustices and your poetry reflects the injustice against both humans and animals. Why are you so responsive to such cruelty, and do you believe that poets can be effective in social change?

SS: *A friend once told me that I am too impressionable, but really, I find the world a very dysfunctional place and cruelty is always with us. We only need to turn on the news to confirm that. Also, we are here for a very short time and most people find it difficult to have much influence. I fervently believe that if you harm or maim another, you also harm or maim a part of yourself. So, I feel strongly about speaking out against any kind of social injustice. Our planet must be held sacred rather than exploited. I see this struggle depicted very clearly in one of my favorite films, "Fitzcarraldo," directed by Werner Herzog with Klaus Kinski where characters face incredible odds.*

BIO: **Silvia Scheibli's** poems were translated into Spanish for the anthology, *La Adelfa Amarga: Six Poets of North America*, edited by Miguel Angel Zapata and published in Lima, Peru. Other anthologies include: *Internal Weather: New Poems, New Poets*, edited by Fred Wolven; *Mantras: an Anthology of Immanentist Poetry* edited by Alan Britt; *New Generation: Poetry*, edited by Fred Wolven; *The Immanentist Anthology: Art of the Superconscious*, published by The Smith/Villiers, Ltd.: New York and London. Her poems have appeared in magazines such as, *Ann Arbor Review, The Bitter Oleander, Black Moon: Poetry of Imagination, The Midwest Quarterly, The Raw Seed Review,* and *Truck*. She is one of many talented poets participating in the **We Are You Project International** (www.weareyouproject.org). She has read everywhere, including Tampa, San Francisco, Half Moon Bay, La Honda, CA, and at Tubac, Arizona's **Geodesic Dome Gallery**.

Alan Britt

Photo by Charles P. Hayes

Five Questions for Alan Britt:

1) You have lived in Baltimore for quite a while. What attracted you about the city compared to Florida where you grew up?

AB: *We moved to Florida from Indiana and Kentucky when I was four. So, I traded snow and four seasons for a warm and muggy climate. Some folks refer to it as a* temperate *climate, but Florida summers without air conditioning are downright hot. I did, however, spend a considerable part of my childhood roaming the wild woods around West Palm Beach, communing with palmettoes, chameleons, snakes, birds and wildflowers, which shaped my sensibility and caused me to fall in love with the lush nature of my new tropical home. But the day I attended the Graduate*

111

Writing Seminars at Johns Hopkins, I reveled in the fact that I'd be living near legitimate art museums! Tampa, at that time, had none. I remember the day I first laid eyes on paintings by Redon, Vermeer, Rembrandt and Goya at the National Gallery. What joy! While I still prefer living close to nature out in suburbia, I am fortunate to enjoy the cultures of Washington, D.C., Baltimore, Philadelphia and New York City, plus a little snow.

2) When you are not teaching at Towson University or writing poems, what do you do to renew yourself?

AB: Academic responsibilities during semesters can overwhelm and limit time and energy for creativity. I am fortunate, however, to teach many poetry writing classes which allow me the opportunity to study and share books by a variety of talented poets. Otherwise, I enjoy an occasional stroll through nature, and when I can, I'll hunker in my basement with music plus a glass or two of wine to enter the glorious zone of imagination.

3) People in general have a difficult time juggling family & work. On top of these commitments, poets need time to write. How do you set priorities?

AB: True, as Wordsworth announced, the world is indeed too much with us. But creativity is a priority. It is more important to my spiritual evolution than writing checks to crooks who supply us with gas and electric, so I insist on creative time. Problem is, the "world" could care less about my creative time and, thus, intrudes.

4) How has the new technology—ezines, blogs, websites, social web pages—influenced your thinking about publishing your poems?

AB: Web publishing is quick, sometimes immediate. Editors often respond in minutes rather than months. Because it's less expensive and doesn't require support from academic and grant institutions, there is an incredible variety of zines on the Web. The web is open to experimentation. I would write what I desire to write regardless of venues for publication, but the Web affords more options for publishing my work.

5. Do you think that poets can be effective in social changes?

AB: I do not think poets effect much if any social change. We inhabit such a calloused culture in the US. Folks are interested in accumulating things, not in cultivating their sensibilities. My occasional yawps are mostly therapeutic.

BIO: **Alan Britt's** interview at **The Library of Congress** for *The Poet and the Poem* (http://www.loc.gov/poetry/poetpoem.html#alan-britt) aired on **Pacifica Radio** in January 2013. His interview with *Minnesota Review* is up at http://minnesotareview.wordpress.com/. He read poems at the **World Trade Center/Tribute WTC Visitor Center** in Manhattan/NYC, April 2012 and the **Maysles Cinema** in Harlem/NYC, February 2013. His latest books are *Alone with the Terrible Universe* (2011), *Greatest Hits* (2010), *Hurricane* (2010), *Vegetable Love* (2009), *Vermilion* (2006), *Infinite Days* (2003), *Amnesia Tango* (1998) and *Bodies of Lightning* (1995). He is Poetry Editor for the **We Are You Project International** (www.weareyouproject.org) and Book Review Editor for *Ragazine* (http://ragazine.cc/). Alan teaches English/Creative Writing at Towson University and lives in Reisterstown, Maryland with his wife, daughter, two Bouviers des Flandres, one Bichon Frise and two formally feral cats.

THE BITTER OLEANDER
Library of Poetry

BITTER OLEANDER
P R E S S

Torn Apart by Joyce Mansour —translated by Serge Gavronsky	$14.00
Children of the Quadrilateral by Benjamin Péret —translated by Jane Barnard & Albert Frank Moritz	$14.00
Edible Amazonia by Nicomedes Suárez-Araúz —translated by Steven Ford Brown	$11.00
A Cage of Transparent Words by Alberto Blanco —a bilingual edition showcasing multiple translators—	$20.00
Afterglow/Tras el rayo by Alberto Blanco —translated by Jennifer Rathbun	$21.00
Of Flies and Monkeys/De singes et de mouches by Jacques Dupin —translated by John Taylor	$24.00
1001 Winters by Kristiina Ehin —translated by Ilmar Lehtpere	$21.00
The Moon Rises in the Rattlesnake's Mouth by Silvia Scheibli	$ 6.00
Half-Said by Paul B. Roth	$10.00
Cadenzas by Needlelight by Paul B. Roth	$16.00
On Carbon-Dating Hunger by Anthony Seidman	$14.00
Festival of Stone by Steve Barfield	$12.00
Infinite Days by Alan Britt	$16.00
Teaching Bones to Fly by Christine Boyka Kluge	$14.00
Travel Over Water by Ye Chun	$14.00
Where Thirsts Intersect by Anthony Seidman	$16.00
Vermilion by Alan Britt	$16.00
Stirring the Mirror by Christine Boyka Kluge	$16.00
Gold Carp Jack Fruit Mirrors by George Kalamaras	$18.00
Van Gogh in Poems by Carol Dine	$21.00
Giving Way by Shawn Fawson	$16.00
If Night is Falling by John Taylor	$16.00
The First Decade: 1968-1978 by *Duane Locke*	$25.00
Empire in the Shade of a Grass Blade by Rob Cook	$18.00

All back issues and single copies of *The Bitter Oleander* are available for $10.00
For more information, contact us at info@bitteroleander.com
or visit us on Facebook or at
www.bitteroleander.com